Endpapers.
Snowstorm.
Life in the regions north of the Arctic Circle is hard, yet
towns still grow up in the land of the Midnight Sun.
Norilsk, the most northerly town in the Soviet Union,
today has a population of 129,000.

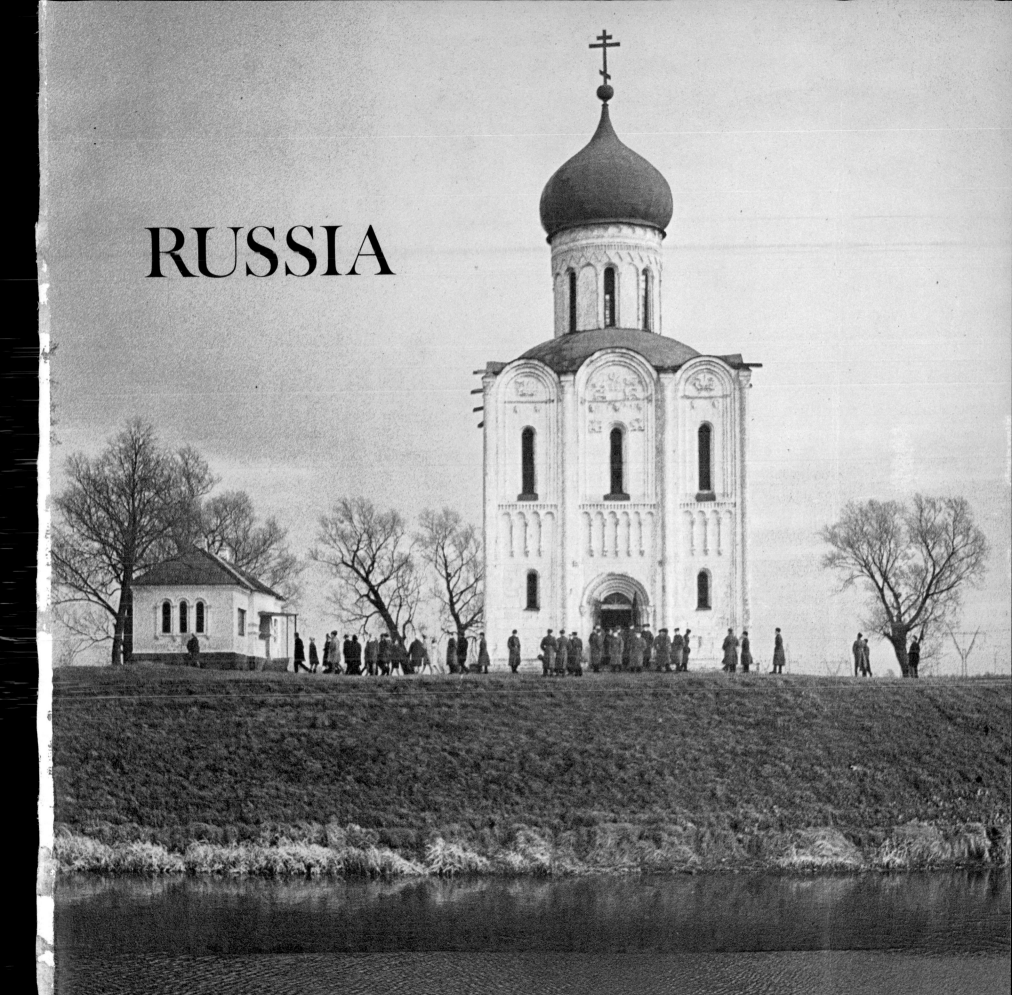

RUSSIA

RUSSIA

by Marianne Sinclair
with introductions by
Heinrich Böll and Valentin Katayev

Simon and Schuster   New York

Illustrations and introductions © 1970 by Belser Verlag Stuttgart
Text © 1976 by Marshall Cavendish Publications Limited
All rights reserved including the right of reproduction in whole or in part in any form
Published in the United States by Simon and Schuster
A Gulf+Western Company
Rockefeller Center, 630 Fifth Avenue,
New York, New York 10020

Editor: Gabrielle Weaver
ISBN 0-671-22433-6
Library of Congress Catalog Card Number 76-15844
Printed in Great Britain

Introduction

Everyone is aware of the vastness of the USSR, but few people know of the diversity of climate, race, culture and history in this land. The many differences between the peoples of the USSR and the environments in which they live, accentuate the startling achievements of the Russian people in the years since the revolution.

Whatever one's political persuasions, one cannot but be impressed by the tenacity and unity of spirit which has led to the development and improvement in all aspects of Russian life in so short a span of time. These can be seen in the large scale industrialization and the harnessing of energy sources, the developments in food production and transportation, the giant leap forward in science and technology and of course the astonishing achievements in space exploration.

This book is not only a pictorial record of these achievements, but also a tribute to the breathtaking beauty of the landscapes of the USSR: from the sparse Siberian Taiga to the pine forests of the West, from snow-capped mountains to the Karakum desert. The illustrations show also the architecture of the cities as a subtle blend of eastern and western influences, of historic cupolas and space-age symmetry, of the exotic and the functional. It is these features of the USSR which have inspired Nobel prize-winner Heinrich Böll to write his moving introduction to this beautiful book and to which the peoples of Russia may point with justifiable pride.

*This page: Red Square with
Lenin's tomb on the left.
Next page: Memories in the
Heroes' Cemetery of Pisaryovo, where
many of the 600,000 who died
in the 900-day seige of Leningrad
in the Second World War are buried.*

Photographs by

Lothar Volleh
Max Alpert
Igor Vinogradov
Lew Weissmann
Vadim Gippenreiter
Dmitri Donskoi
Oleg Ivanov
Valentin Lebedyev
Lew Nossow

Alexandr Moklezov
Michail Oserski
Alexandr Opolovnikov
Alexandr Poroshnuakov
Viktor Panov
Eduard Pessov
Nikolai Rachmanov
Vladislav Schidlovski
Valeri Shustov

Mussa Selimchanov
Dmitri Smirnov
Sergej Solovyev
Vsevolod Tarassevitsch
Varfolomej Teterin
Lew Usstinov
Boris Utkin

Contents

Heinrich Böll
'He who has eyes to see, let him see'

First of all, an admission: I am not a great one for sumptuous volumes of photographs, whether the masterpieces they portray in full colour are Danish, Soviet, American, German (East or West) or Czech. Such splendours, however well lit and well photographed, leave me rather cold. My point is that peoples, nations, states, indeed any community, private companies included, have an understandable wish to display what they have achieved, or what history has allocated to them: things as impressive as the Kremlin or the city of Leningrad, or the Cathedral and Roman vaults of Cologne, or as those Italian cities and their sights which you can count off from Verona to Palermo, as though saying prayers for them on a rosary. Next come the economic achievements, prize bulls, prize potatoes, moving pavements, new buildings, underground railways, and then, finally, the inevitable glimpse of the throbbing night-life. There is something childlike in the pride that is taken in this display of sights; it is like a schoolboy who arrives home having come first in every subject, and spreads his report on the table with the words: 'Look, aren't I clever.' Whether it is the mayor or the factory manager getting a medal or the schoolboy getting the money for an ice-cream, beaming faces look on during the congratulations and the presentations and there is something stirring about it all. The faces of politicians and industrialists are bound to light up when they hear something good about themselves.

Perhaps what is called for at this point is a long reflection about what is truly representative, with a detailed appendix about the marking system in schools, but I will spare both myself and the reader. What is distinguished, and therefore outstanding, is rarely representative — it makes no difference whether the distinction is literary or political.

While I am on the subject of admissions, here is another: I find the Kremlin marvellous, Leningrad ravishing, and the Hermitage, both as a building and as an art gallery, past description. I even like going down, once in a while, into the Roman vaults of Cologne. After all, while you are looking at the sights you can also do what really should be done thoroughly in foreign countries and cities, and that is walking around, looking at people. That is how you see not only the sights, but much more besides.

A prestige picture-book inevitably contains nothing but 'firsts' just like those in the school reports of perfect pupils are as problematic as their marks and as the whole system of achievement and assessment. For example, if I had to ignore my conscience and allocate marks, I would give the most to a boy who instead of making 110 mistakes in a dictation, only made 56, although 'objectively' 56 would almost certainly earn him the lowest mark available.

So much for my admissions and prior assumptions. I have a deep suspicion that they apply equally to many authors, painters and film makers, and that they give rise to an appalling amount of misunderstanding and wounded pride, and to just as many witch-hunts, slanders and refutations of slander. Of course, now and again, privately, authors and painters are stirred, stirred even to tears, but the works which they create must not stir. They may move, inwardly – the much maligned word emotion expresses what I mean – but they must never simply stir. Soups and puddings are stirred; batter can be stirred, perhaps to make pancakes or waffles, and in this sense there are some artists who do a great deal of stirring, genre painters for example. But there is nothing about Moscow that is stirring, nor about that much maligned city, blessed by the grime of centuries, Cologne, while there is much about both that is moving. What matters in this context is the material, physical difference between the capacity to stir and the capacity to move.

If I had the time and the opportunity, a highly skilled and sensitive cameraman and enough high quality colour film I would like to make two films. The first would be played by the people on the streets of Moscow. It would be a film with some two million stars, and with no sights in the traditional sense, although it is possible that I would allow the Kremlin a quick inconsequential glance over the shoulders of the people on Moscow's streets and squares. There would be no cars in my film, only pedestrians, those constant streams of millions of people on the move, who to me are more than just a mass. It might even suffice to drive very slowly with my back to the Kremlin, panning a camera along the mile long queue of people waiting on Red Square to catch a glimpse of the embalmed body of Lenin. At first I would only take faces, then legs, then hands, eventually whole bodies and then finally faces again. Such a film would probably strike most people as indescribably monotonous, because, even though their main occupation is seeing, they have forgotten the words of the Bible: *He who has eyes to see, let him see.* Someone ought subsequently to make similar films about London, New York, East and West Berlin, Rome and Peking, after which we might be closer to knowing what Soviet, British or American citizens are really like. I have an idea for a film of utopia: it would show a million Russians walking around New York, a million Americans in Moscow, a million Germans in Peking. That would be the only true and acceptable form of invasion and the only possible meaning of what we call international understanding and which ought one day to turn into real understanding between peoples.

In this context a book like this one is always welcome, for it serves to open people's eyes, to set aside their prejudices and to prepare them for future visits to a country which is still as strange to us as we are to it. Besides I am still and will always be prepared to make that allowance which the USSR and her peoples are always being denied, although their history entitles them to it: an allowance for the measureless destruction, crime and murder that was committed on Soviet territory between 1941 and 1945. This handicap, as yet unquantified, gives another dimension to the achievements of the USSR.Her 'firsts' are more than stirring, they are moving. As far as I wish to make a film about the faces and hands of Soviet citizens (I would probably have to leave their legs out of it, because in order to keep the superciliousness and snobbery of a Western audience within reasonable proportions I would have to provide a sociological, philosophical and theological study of clothing (with special reference to footwear) in the light of the east-west détente), but still, if I wish to make such a film it is only because for me the real sights of a country are her people and their faces.

The second film I would like to make, given the same technical conditions, would cover all the stages and variations of the spring thaw in Moscow after a long hard winter: a film ranging from pure white snow to that oily yellow and black mess of what might once have been snow and which is heaped up alongside the main roads leading out of Moscow. All sorts and conditions of snow, aristocratic snow, proletarian bourgeois snow, classless snow, sacred snow, insulted and injured snow, street snow and back yard snow. I would show how snow lying on small side roads with little traffic is trodden and driven to ice, wihle at the same time the great boulevards and prospects are clean and free of snow. The film would of course have to record how the vastly interesting technical problems caused by snow and ice in a city the size of Moscow are solved: where is the man responsible for snow and ice in Moscow, what is his name, how large is the army of workers at his disposal, who invented those machines rather reminiscent of ships' propellers and designed to sweep up the snow on to conveyor belts which in turn dump it in lorries? Has he, may we ask, received a medal for his invention? What if it snows at night, just after the main streets have finally been cleared and when the man in charge is on his way to bed? Does his face cloud over as he looks worriedly at the sky? Does the innocent white snow make him swear as he picks up the telephone to mobilize those machines which roll out three or four at a time to lift the burden of this heaven-sent innocence from the great boulevards?

The fascination of Moscow during the thaw comes from the simultaneous nature of so many different stages of winter. While great mountains of snow remain in the courtyards, as if stored there for a period of shortage, spring has already broken on the

9

streets. In streets shaded from the sun women hack away at two foot thick sheets of ice while a few hundred yards away people are sitting out in the sunshine. In one street people are shivering with cold, yet a few hundred yards further on they take off their coats. Finally, there is the water, dripping from roofs, pouring off hills and slopes into streets lower down, following the inexorable laws of nature, then forming puddles, building up at blocked drains, making miniature lakes in the slightest dip or hollow.

The finalé of the film would be the inevitable look down into the main drains where gurgling dirty floods of water, formed of snow which was once white as snow, but now mixed with dirt and dust from the streets and roofs of Moscow, finally leave the city. A film like this would, by the standards of realism, also contain nothing but 'firsts' – full marks to the chief organizer of the city's snow and ice clearing teams, to the designer of the snow-shovelling conveyor-belts, to the women who shovel snow from the roofs and to the men who keep the streets down below closed to protect passers-by, and of course to the engineers who designed and built the drains and sewers which carry the melted snow to oblivion. A film like this would undoubtedly have to be in colour, and it would, I fear, come across as an abstract, non-representational composition, although it would contain nothing fictitious but only an organised version of what is commonly called reality. Perhaps this film, made up only of composition and without artifice, would serve to counter some foolish prejudices about art. It would also furnish a well-earned memorial to snows of Russia and of Moscow, to Soviet snow. The long hard winter may seem a curse to many Russians but on two occasions it has undoubtedly been a blessing, in 1812 and in 1941. Last of all, this film should not, on materialist rather than metaphysical grounds, ignore the heavens, which always provide snow when it is 'historically' necessary. Both these films I have in mind would, I believe, not be stirring, but moving.

I must add a few words about those authors and writers who insist on having their look into the sewers. We so readily suspect those whose ambition is to see only the dirt, the slums, the cripples – the unrepresentative. For those remarkable people something else is representative, that incomprehensible thing we call life and which is interpreted by everyone in a different way, just as reality is. The writer, who insists, both literally and metaphorically, on looking into the sewers, is, in the true sense, a realist, even if he is making abstract films about snow and Moscow. Snow in cities inevitably turns into dirty water, and this is a blessing, for people would not enjoy spending their whole lives in clean white snow. It would be an artificial life if the snow stayed pure for ever.

Valentin Katayev 'Forward, faster than time'

People of my generation have lived through violent times. Their lives have been so crammed with world-shattering events that it would take hundreds, even thousands of books and millions of feet of film to record them all in detail. The fate of the Russian people has been particularly hard. We have been through cruel and bloody wars, and more than one revolution. But, against all the odds, my generation, a whole generation of Russians, did not succumb. Although we were crippled by World War I the October Revolution rescued us and put us on our feet again. What I am now, my whole life and all I have done, I owe exclusively to the Revolution. I am a child of the Revolution, a wayward child perhaps, but still its child.

The Great October Revolution transformed our backward country into a powerful socialist state. The summer of 1919, when the Civil War in the Ukraine was at its fiercest, is still clear in my mind. Our military train, equipped with old green three-inch guns, was in Losovaya. White acacias were in bloom. There had just been a thunderstorm. We were very close to the front. The soldiers, with many sailors among them, stood in the doors of the carriages which were decorated with acacias. A band played the Internationale. A bright violet rainbow stood out against the background of a dark bank of cloud and it seemed as if our train was heading into a great transparent gateway, sharply outlined before us . . .

When the Civil War came to an end, terrible destruction and poverty covered the whole country. The streets of Moscow were blocked by snowdrifts. There was no light in the houses and no food in the shops. It was then that Herbert Wells, the Englishman, visited Russia. He thought the end had come. Lenin received the famous writer, who thought Russia's only salvation lay in English pounds and American dollars and that the country would sink if English and American help were refused. Like Wells, Lenin saw the destruction and the destitution, but where Wells only had eyes for the end, Lenin could see the new beginning. Lenin saw, as early as that, a country bright with electric lights, a country of rich harvests and factory chimneys pouring forth smoke. With neither pounds nor dollars to help them, our people began to build.

The heroic days of the First Five-Year-Plan spring to my mind. I was then employed in the building of Magnitogorsk. I remember the parched, desolate steppe, the new railway line and the single carriage with a bell on the roof, which was the original station for the future town of Magnitogorsk. The sun was hidden by columns of smoke and soot. The wind tore down our tents and carried them off into the steppe. It seemed so unlikely that in a few years there would be on this site a vast steelworks, the biggest blast furnaces in the world, a coke and chemical combine, a socialist city. But the Soviet workers there could already see in their mind's eye gardens flourishing on the parched steppe and their reflections in wide canals.

Untamed nature does not appeal to me. I am frightened by uncharted seas. Dark forests and solitary peaks sadden me. Nature is made only beautiful by the presence and activity of human beings, using their reason and unbending will to transform the world. A steamer on the open sea, a lighthouse on a rocky cliff, a mountaineer conquering Elbrus, a motor road across the Taiga, a dam holding back a river, a cotton plantation, green fields under cultivation, a canal in the desert. These for me are the true beauties of nature. Nature is the most conservative force in our country, and in the building of Communism we completely transformed nature, bending her to our own needs.

I count myself lucky to have been a witness of all the revolutionary changes in the Russian Soviet state. One of my earliest childhood memories is of the long thin pine splinters that on long winter evenings were used, in the absence of candles or oil-lamps, to light the peasant cottages scattered over the snowbound vastness of Russia. What has recently impressed me most deeply has been the triumphant success of Soviet astronauts in their historic journeys into space. From splinters of pine to flights by Soviet spacecraft, that is the span of our country's development over an incredibly short period of time. Mayakovsky once coined the slogan 'Forward, faster than time.' This summons became reality. Life has overtaken time here and daily moves further ahead. But what energy and what mighty efforts this victory over time has cost the Soviet people!

As I turn the pages of this book, absorbed in its pictures, I relive many experiences from my past life. Moscow, 30th December 1922, five years after the Revolution. The Civil War was over and we were celebrating the foundation of the Union of Soviet Socialist Republics. What a beautiful city Moscow was on that day. The Kremlin hovered in the limpid mist of driving snow. The chimes of the clock rang out crystal clear from the ancient tower of the Redeemer, hailing the victorious birth of the first socialist federation in the world. Moscow in those days was still, by outward appearances, an old city. Jackdaws circled around the steep gabled roofs of the bell-towers and the golden cupolas of the churches and chapels. The golden eagle of the Tsars still glittered on the Kremlin towers. The Kitaigorod wall with its rounded gates and their lizard-green tiles still encircled the Old Square. But the old aura of aristocrats and merchants was already gone. A new soul had been born, free, socialist, unfettered.

A new and different Moscow has grown and flourished before our eyes. 48 years of Soviet power have changed the city beyond recognition. It is difficult while walking along the streets, to recall what they were like before; we have quickly become accustomed to the new Moscow, to Gorki Street, the bridges, the metro, Dynamo Stadium, the granite embankments, the electric trains, the asphalt, the lights, the skyscrapers. It sometimes seems as though it was always like that.

No book, not even a hundred books, could ever show their readers what the Soviet State and the Soviet people are really like. As Goethe said, the artist is always confronted by the many-headed hydra of reality, the greatest danger facing all writers and painters. And photographers, too. You cannot conceive the inconceivable. But, if you aim to express on each and every page as much as possible of what is really significant, then you can, according to the law by which quantity becomes quality, convey something about historical phenomena. The photographs in this book impressed me deeply, for they record not only our glorious architectural monuments, but also our recent achievements, monuments erected by our people to the incredible growth of our culture, art, science and technology, our civilization.

Moscow: history and development

The Moscow which the three sisters yearned after in Chekhov's play looked very different from the Moscow of today. In Dickens' time, London was a modern city but Moscow at the turn of the century had not been a capital for 200 years and had still a distinctly provincial air about it. It was mockingly known to the sophisticated St. Petersburgers as 'Russia's biggest village' and until quite recently many of its houses were still built of wood in the traditional *izba* style. However, all this has changed. When the Bolsheviks made Moscow their capital in March 1918, it was a rundown city of less than 1,000,000 people. Today, it has a population of over 7,000,000 and little is left of its provincial character. As the centre of the largest country in the world, the leading city of the socialist world and the capital of a super-power, Moscow has had to do a lot of growing and expanding in order to keep up with the economic development of the Soviet Union over the last fifty years.

Although the onion domes of Moscow's churches are still the most familiar images the West has of the city, we must be convinced of its modern character by the fact that well over half the buildings and monuments depicted in the following photographs were built during the last fifty years: The Lenin Mausoleum, Lomonosov University, the Moscow Underground, the Comecon building, the skyscraper blocks of offices and flats along Kalinin Prospect, The Rossiya Hotel, the Cosmonauts' Monument. These are the new landmarks of Moscow, shown as proudly to the visiting foreigner as the more traditional sights of the Kremlin, the Spassky Tower and the Cathedral of Basil the Blessed. After all, which book on Paris, Rome or London would contain so great a proportion of modern buildings? Yet this is wholly appropriate to Moscow and we would certainly get a distorted picture if only the more ancient and picturesque buildings of the Soviet capital were represented.

We notice the intrusion of the modern even in the photographs of the older landmarks; a skyscraper peeping over the traditional buildings, the delicate tracery of cranes above the gilded domes and the towers of the Kremlin, the long, thin shadow cast by Moscow's great needle across the leafy, old-fashioned quarter far below. But the most striking contrasts of all is surely in the strange juxtaposition of the quaint and fussy old church totally dominated by the clean functional lines of the vast Hotel Rossiya. This combination of old and new, the new overshadowing the old and yet including and seeming almost to protect it, captures the essence of today's Moscow, with its respect for the past but its very definite accent on the present.

Moscow was founded over 800 years ago and was at first contained within the walled area of the Kremlin. The original wooden walls which made the Kremlin a fortified city were soon replaced by stone ones and the city of Moscow itself eventually spilled over into the outlying districts. It was a trading centre, strategically located in the heart of the enormous Russian wooded plain, and it grew so much in size and importance that by the mid-sixteenth century, it was larger than London. The streets radiated like the spokes of a wheel from the gates of the Kremlin walls. Most of the houses were of wood with few brick constructions and much of the city was destroyed by fire when Napoleon's army occupied it in 1812.

Moscow lost much of its political importance when Peter the Great transferred his capital in 1712 to the new town of St. Petersburg on the Baltic. But it remained a large industrial and trading centre, as well as an important centre of art and learning. When, in the nineteenth century, factories and textile mills grew up on the outskirts of Moscow, the new prosperity this brought to the city was recorded in the theatres, picture galleries and fine houses that were built around this time. Many of these structures, including the Bolshoi Theatre, are still to be admired today; the slums in which the proletariat then lived have since disappeared.

Although, with over two-thirds of Moscovites living in new dwellings, Moscow is predominately modern in appearance, its heart remains the Kremlin with all its relics of the city's history and past. The Kremlin is also the seat of the present government. Moscow itself, as one writer put it, is like Mecca to a Moslem; a pilgrimage to Moscow is a 'must' for every Soviet man and woman: 'Moscow means everything to a Russian, but it also means a great deal to a Yakut or a Chukchi six thousand miles away in the frozen Siberian wilderness.' And indeed, foreign visitors are struck by the sheer variety of faces, costumes and types to be seen milling about Red Square or visiting the Kremlin on any day of the week. Every type of regional costume, from town and from country, from hot and cold lands, can be found; some visitors are Asiatic, some have European features, all range in age from schoolchildren to white-bearded patriarchs. Soviet citizens come from all parts of the Soviet Union to pay tribute to the beauty and historical importance of their capital; their love for Moscow has played an important part in welding them together and in creating a feeling of unity in so varied and vast a land.

Page 16
The entrance to the Kremlin. In order to reach the interior of the walled area of the Kremlin, visitors must pass over Trinity Bridge.

Page 17
Once inside the walled area of the Kremlin our picture shows a view of the Cathedral Square. This lies between the three finest cathedrals of the Kremlin and the belfry of Ivan the Great which dominates the group and the Kremlin palace. The palace was built by the German architect Konstantin Thon from 1838 to 1849, for Tsar Nicholas I. The Tsar so valued the view that he arranged for the demolition of the fine sixteenth-century church of St. John the Baptist, as it obscured his view from the palace of the Cathedral of the Saviour.

Pages 18-19
On Red Square.
On the left are the tomb of Lenin and some of the towers of the Kremlin.
On the right is the Historical Museum, designed by an English architect named Sherwood in 1875. He chose a pseudo-Russian style of architecture. The museum contains more than 300,000 exhibits which illustrate the most striking events in Russian history.

Page 20
Changing of the Guard at the entrance to the Lenin Mausoleum.

Pages 22-23
Evening in Moscow.
Sunset over the towers and domes of the Kremlin.

Pages 24-25
In the Lenin Stadium.
Sportsmen and women from every Soviet Republic take part in the great sporting occasion known as the 'Spartakiada'.

Moscow: capital city and political centre

If you had never been to New York and for some reason could only spend an hour there, you might elect to go to the Rockefeller Plaza for a quick, atmospheric glimpse of the sky-scraper city; in London, you would probably opt for Piccadilly Circus or Trafalgar Square; in Paris you might hesitate between the Champs-Elysées and a stroll along the Seine. In Moscow, you would go to only one place in that brief span of time: Red Square. The main difference between Red Square and the sights of New York or London is that Rockefeller Plaza or Piccadilly Circus are quite apolitical and it is unlikely that you would think for a moment about the governmental systems of those countries. In Red Square, you would be reminded at every step and glance of the political system of the Soviet Union and its recent history.

The first thing you would see in Red Square would be the endless queue of people waiting to go into the red marble Mausoleum, which houses the embalmed body of Lenin, founder of Russian Communism. Just above the entrance to the Mausoleum, you would recognize from newspaper photographs the long balcony on which Soviet State and Party leaders stand during anniversary celebrations. Behind the Mausoleum, you would see the high walls of the Kremlin which is linked so indissolubly with the present government, in the popular imagination, that Soviet leaders are often called 'The men inside the Kremlin.' On one side of the square you would see conducted parties of Russian schoolchildren in red pioneer scarves, patiently waiting to go into the State Historical Museum, decorated with pictures of Marx, Engels and Lenin. At your feet you would notice long white lines painted on the grey stone slabs; these lines are there to guide the steps of the hundreds of thousands of soldiers, workers and athletes who march across the square during the May Day and November 7th parades. During your hour in Red Square, your elbow would probably be jogged several times by urchins trying to sell you almost the only 'souvenirs' of Moscow available: a badge with Lenin's profile on it or a hammer and sickle pin. Thus you cannot help but be reminded of politics in Red Square, where strangely the only non-political facet is its name. It has been called *Red Square* since the seventeenth century, not for the reason that red is the traditional colour of the Socialist flag, but because the word *red* means 'beautiful' in old Slavic.

Why is Moscow so political a capital? Perhaps because the system itself is by definition more pervasive than that in the West. The socialist form of government expects to play a fuller role in the lives of its citizens and to control far-ranging aspects of their daily lives, just as it expects those citizens to participate far more actively in the life of the government than would be the case in a non-socialist state. The distinctly political flavour of Moscow is a reflection of the general political ambiance which prevails in the country as a whole.

Moscow itself is a capital twice over. It is the capital of the Russian Federation and the capital of the entire Soviet Union. The Russian Federation, or Russia proper, is just one of the fifteen constituent republics which make up the vast Union of Socialist Soviet Republics, founded by the Bolsheviks in 1922. This multi-national and multi-lingual union covers one-sixth of the earth's land surface, which makes for an almost infinite variety in climate, topography, flora, fauna, races and customs. The Soviet Union is a socialist state of workers and peasants; the state owns and controls the means of production, e.g. all the natural resources, the factories, the banks, the means of transport and communication, the large state-organized agricultural enterprises, most of the dwelling houses in the cities, etc. The Communist Party dominates the state system; as the most authoritative public organization, it has exerted power and controlled the system since 1917, when the Tsarist regime was swept away and the first Socialist or Marxist-Leninist nation was born.

Socialism in the USSR is about sixty years old; although over a third of that time has been spent in devastating wars or in exhaustive post-war reconstruction, the country has made gigantic strides since the days when it was a nation of desperately poor people, peasants and workers with a 70 per cent illiteracy rate. Whatever one's views on Communism as a political ideology, there is little doubt that the system has improved the quality of life for millions in the Soviet Union. In half a century, the Soviet Union has become one of the largest industrial powers in the world. It has improved the health, the educational standards and the working conditions of its inhabitants immeasurably. These achievements have meant some sacrifices in the 'standard of living' as measured in capitalist terms of cars, appliances, clothes and services, but this standard of living too has been improved in recent years. Perhaps the Soviet people did once live for the future, toiling for the hypothetical happiness of unborn generations, but they now live most definitely in the present and for their own happiness.

Page 40
The Cosmonauts' Monument.
*The monument, 96 metres high, was erected in honour of
the conquest of space by the Soviet People.*

Page 41
A Military Parade on Red Square.

Page 43
A Metro Station.
*The magnificent décor of the Moscow Underground
Railway illuminated by baroque chandeliers.*

Page 44
Lomonosov University.
*The imposing edifice of Moscow State University on the
Lenin Hills is where 36,000 students pursue their
education.*

Page 45
In a Popular Bookshop.
*Reading both for pleasure and self-improvement is a
popular pastime. Many of the books published in the
USSR run into editions of millions.*

Pages 46-47
The Bolshoi Theatre.
The focal point of the renowned Russian ballet.

Moscow: intellectual and cultural centre

In *The Soul of Man under Socialism*, Oscar Wilde declared that it was not art which should become popular but the people who should strive to become artistic. In the Soviet Union, however, it is not considered to be a matter of either/or. The official cultural policy since the Revolution has been that art should become popular *and* that the people should become artistic. Perhaps in no other country in the world do the arts play so honoured a part in national life, yet the degree of state control over cultural matters can be, and often is, criticized, not only abroad, but also within the Soviet Union itself. Stalin declared that writers should be 'the engineers of soul' and the Soviet Encyclopedia has laid down the rule that artists must produce work which is 'comprehensible to the millions, true to life, and permeated with the ideas of the building of socialism.' This official 'utilitarian' approach to culture can lead to excesses in zeal; as the Soviet poet, Zabolotsky has wittily put it:

> The form of a cow
> Reading a textbook on Butter Making
> Will shine over the infant's bed
> Instead of the Madonna.

However, despite the struggle now being waged between the 'Stalinist' and the 'Liberal' factions in all branches of the arts and the massive publicity of the Pasternak and Solzhenitsyn affairs, we can appreciate the success scored by the regime in making the people 'artistic' so that (according to the well-known English historian, Alexander Werth) they are today 'the best-read, most cultured people in the world'. An ordinary Russian worker is more likely to have read or seen a Shakespeare play than a worker born in Stratford-upon-Avon. He will almost certainly have read many of his own classics, in ridiculously cheap editions, and will have been trained and encouraged from childhood to enjoy classical music, ballet, theatre and visits to museums.

Inevitably, Moscow is the intellectual and cultural centre of the Soviet Union, although Leningrad is still a serious rival which, in the past, often surpassed the capital in cultural achievements and fame. Everyone has heard of the Bolshoi Ballet and the Moscow Arts Theatre, while Prokofiev, Shostakovitzh, Oistrach and Gillels are household names to classical music-lovers throughout the world. It is fitting in a land where dancing and music are so much the essence of the traditional 'Russian Soul,' that it should be these art forms which have found such a high degree of excellence and popularity in the Soviet Union of today. The popularity of the theatre

(94,000,000 theatre seats sold in the USSR in 1961: almost one for every other inhabitant) is partly traditional and partly due to the creation of special Children's Theatres which kindle an interest in seeing good plays from early childhood. There are several of these in Moscow.

In theatre, ballet and opera, the classics are tremendously popular, as audiences do not want only themes which exalt 'the pathos of labour', as Khrushchev maintained all good modern works of art should do. But the great themes of the October Revolution, the heroic struggle against Hitler's invading armies and present-day Soviet space exploits are also often to be seen. Like the contemporary Chinese operas which are better known in the West, the content and message of these plays and ballets may seem a trifle naïve or even distasteful to Western tastes; their strong patriotic flavour is no longer fashionable in Europe; yet we can unreservedly admire their stylistic sophistication and the flawless execution of their complex choreography.

The definition of culture is very broad in the Soviet Union; even activities like sports, chess or gymnastics fall into this category, as does the circus, which is looked upon as entertainment rather than culture in the West. But the Soviet circus, especially the Moscow State Circus is much more artistic and 'cultural' than in other countries. Outstanding circus performers are as highly paid and respected as top theatre and film actors. As in other Soviet cities, there are also 'parks of recreation and culture' in Moscow, the most famous one being the Gorky Recreation Park. These parks are authentic cultural centres, since they contain cinemas, theatres, open air stages, lecture rooms, libraries and travelling art exhibitions. It is to such parks that the foreign visitor should go to observe the nature of culture in the Soviet Union. Let him also remember to visit a few bookshops and museums. Even if he cannot read the Russian titles, he can read the expressions of concentration and eagerness on the faces of the students and workers who have come to buy the books. When he gets tired of looking at the paintings in the galleries, he will find it fascinating to study the crowds of *kholkozians* and old *babushkas* who have come to admire works of art.

Pages 50-51
Moscow State Circus.
Its performers are honoured and respected artistes in the USSR.
Left: The great trapeze act.
Right: Popov the Clown and Liver, his dog.

Pages 52-53
In the Tretyakov Art Gallery.
The Tretyakov Gallery, like other Soviet museums, houses world-famous treasures, viewed and admired daily by countless visitors.

Page 55
'October Suite'.
A performance by the Bolshoi Ballet in memory of the October Revolution.

Page 56
The Great Crown of the Tsars.
Showpiece of the diamond collection housed in the
Kremlin Armoury. The crown weighs 2.25 kilograms and
is bedecked with 4936 diamonds totalling 2858 carats.

Page 58
Portrait of a famous Soviet Musician.
The cellist Mstislav Rostropovich, honoured as a
'Peoples Artist of the Soviet Union'.

Page 59
Moscow's 'Theatre of Agitation'.
A performance to celebrate the New Year in the theatre
of the Leninist Young Communist League.

Leningrad, Petrograd and Petersburg

Many poets have written odes to their native city, but Alexander Pushkin's verses reflect the unusual, almost unique degree of attachment which Leningraders feel for their city and their obsession with its beauty:

I love you so, oh Peter's creature
For your severe and noble face!
For the river's flow so majestic
For her embankments stone-encased,
For your grille railings' matchless lace...

Often referred to as 'The Northern Palmyra' or the 'Venice of the North', Leningrad richly deserves its reputation; but whereas the original Venice must compete with the equally high reputation of its neighbours, Florence and Rome, Leningrad is unquestionably the handsomest city in the whole of the Soviet Union. The Leningraders are very conscious of this distinction and they feel specially privileged to live there. Some have even attributed this patriotic pride in the city's beauty to the fact that it did not fall into German hands during World War II. For instance, Leningraders knew that the Nazis planned to destroy their city if it fell in World War II and they preferred to starve and suffer the most atrocious privations during the 900-day siege, rather than allow this to happen.

The city was founded by Peter the Great in 1703; it was to be his capital, his seaport and naval base on the Baltic and his 'window into Europe'. It was designed by the most celebrated European architects of the eighteenth and nineteenth centuries, who had at their disposal unlimited labour and unlimited funds. Countless stonemasons and labourers were brought to the damp and foggy marshes of the Neva Delta, close to the Arctic Circle, to slave away at building Peter's city. As is so often the case when wonders of the world are built at the whim of princes, tens of thousands died in the process and are buried in anonymous graves below the foundations of the city which they helped to fashion with their bare hands. The result is a city of matchless beauty built on 105 islands and spanned by some 700 bridges, containing over 2,500 buildings and monuments considered to be architectural classics, a city from which ugliness and modern construction have been banned. The fact that Leningrad was built so comparatively recently, and in so short a time, means that it has no truly ancient relics of the past; it possesses instead a delightful unity of style.

Leningrad suffered from constant shelling during its siege. The famous Peteroff palace and its legendary gardens were among the places devastated by the Germans. The great cascade had turned into an 'arctic precipice' and there was a 'gaping hole where once Samson rested among the fountains'. But the Leningraders were determined that their city should be rebuilt. As the poet Olga Berggolts declared after visiting the ruined Peteroff:

> *Again from the black dust, from the place*
> *Of death and ashes, will arise the gardens as before.*
> *So will it be. I firmly believe in miracles.*
> *You gave me that belief, my Leningrad.*

And so it was. With devotion and determination, the people of Leningrad lovingly reconstructed their city. Leningrad is not only 'Peter's creature' but very much the creature of its own citizens. It is also important to recall that it is not only a city of Tsars and palaces, but one with strong proud revolutionary associations. The Fortress of Peter and Paul was the first building to be built in the city; it was also the prison which housed Russian revolutionaries throughout the nineteenth century. Leningrad is the city of the 'Decembrists', a group of progressive officers who staged an abortive insurrection against the Tsar in 1825. It is the city of the workers who were mown down by mounted cavalry in the 'Bloody Sunday' massacre of 1905. It is the city to which Lenin returned from exile in 1917; above all it is the city where the armed workers stormed the Winter Palace later in the same year, in the culmination of the struggle which gave birth to the Socialist Revolution.

This is why Leningrad is so often called 'the cradle of the revolution' as its citizens will remind you with as much pride as they will tell you of its world-famous authors: Pushkin, Gogol and Dostoevsky, each of whom immortalized the city in his works.

Since the turn of the century, Leningrad has experienced two revolutions, three wars and two changes of regime. Oddly enough, it has also known two changes of name. It was called St. Petersburg until World War I, when it was rebaptized 'Petrograd', because the earlier name was considered too German. It was then renamed Leningrad after Lenin's death. The supreme paradox is that despite these upheavals, St. Petersburg – Petrograd – Leningrad has changed so little in outward appearance that if Catherine the Great were to return today she would hardly notice any difference; though she might be puzzled by the gentleman with the small pointed beard whose portraits and statues now adorn *her* palaces and *her* gardens. They were not, however, built by her but by the people of Leningrad.

Pages 62-63
Leningrad, Venice of the North.
Branches of the Neva and a network of canals run through the city. Our picture shows the towers and cupolas of the Alexander Nevski Monastery.

Pages 64-65
White Nights of Leningrad are those Summer nights on which the sun dips only briefly beneath the horizon. There is neither daylight nor darkness, only a luminous, shadowless twilight.
Our picture shows a group of fishermen on the banks of the Neva, on the right the Dvorzovy Bridge (which can be raised) and in the background the sharp spire of the Cathedral of St. Peter and St. Paul.

Page 67
Leningrad, City of Peter the Great.
View from the Cathedral of St. Isaac to the Winter Palace and the Neva. In the foreground, the very top of the Admiralty Tower.

Page 68
Peteroff Palace.
The magnificent palace gardens of the 'Russian Versailles', built on the outskirts of the city. The Samson Canal runs through the gardens to the sea. Devastated during the many upheavals of the city it has always been restored.

Page 69
Armoured Cruiser 'Aurora', whose guns gave the signal to begin the October Revolution. The ship now lies anchored at the Neva Quay as a memorial to her crew's heroic act.

Pages 70-71
Leningrad, City of the Revolution.
After the storming of the Winter Palace by armed workers
and Red Guards on November 7th 1917, the Soviets
seized power in Petrograd.
Our picture shows revolution celebrations by night on
Palace Square.

Page 72
Russian Birches.
Loved by the people and celebrated in their songs as
symbols of youth and beauty.

Pages 74-75
Palace Square.
View from the Winter Palace to the former Headquarters
of the Army General Staff. The Alexander Column in the
centre of the square celebrates the victory over Napoleon.

Page 76
The Hall of the Malachites in the Winter Palace, built in
the eighteenth century by Rastrelli and conveying an
impression of the splendour of life for the St. Petersburg
Emperors.

Page 77
The Schoolteacher.
Natalya Sergeyevna explains the woodland flora to her
pupils.

Early Russian Art and Religion

In Russia, art and religion are so closely linked that it is impossible to talk of one without referring to the other. The history of painting, sculpture, and architecture in Russia is the history of its churches and monasteries. Certainly until the eighteenth century and perhaps even later, Russian artists found their inspiration chiefly in religious themes and they turned to the Greek Orthodox Church for patronage.

In a sense, early Russian art was 'utilitarian' just as today's socialist art is required to be: art for art's sake did not exist as a concept. Art was a means to an end and that end was to exalt religious fervour in the faithful and to express devotion to the Church and all it stood for. The icons to be found in every Russian home, from the most ornate palace to the humblest peasant's hut, were not there for decoration. They served as shrines for the daily prayers and as constant reminders of spiritual values. The church was usually the tallest and most brightly coloured building in town and village; its vivid domes would remind the flock of its presence and of its ascendancy over their lives. The Tsar himself could not have been more richly arrayed than the patriarch who wore the cape with 1,200,000 pearls woven into its fabric which is displayed in one of the Kremlin museums.

When people are first exposed to the cumulative impact of Russian religious art, they tend to use the expression 'barbaric' to describe its dazzling use of colour, gilt and gems and the elaborateness of its patterns and shapes. Although Russian art developed a unique style of its own, it is a reminder that Russian Christianity originated in the Greek Orthodox faith, which was strongly influenced artistically by the East: this is not surprising as the seat of the church was Constantinople. Anyone who has studied early Greek icons or seen the towers of St. Sophia in present-day Istanbul will easily recognize their influence on Russian holy images and on the domes and cupolas of Russian churches. The representation of the principal figures of the Christian religion, their lack of expressions and their wooden gestures, as well as the inclusion of many allegorical allusions, are closely akin to those found in Byzantine art. What is often striking in Russian icons is that the figures of Christ, the Saints and the Virgin have distinctly Greek or Oriental faces; their large, dark eyes, their aquiline noses and long, oval faces are very unlike the Slavic or Northern cast of features; this can be seen clearly in the sixteenth-century icon of the Madonna [page 84] which is typical in subject and composition, just as the disproportionately large mother's head and the stiff, blessing gesture of her child are also characteristic of Russian iconography.

The way in which icons were painted altered very little over the centuries; unlike religious art in the West, their style remained static. What varied greatly, however, was the amount of gilt used on them and the introduction of gold and silver frames, which gradually encroached on the pictures until they all but covered them. The use of gold on icons was not merely a sign of opulence; it had a symbolic meaning as well. If the artist wished to bring out the humanity of Christ, he would use only colour, but if he wanted to emphasize the regal and godly nature of Jesus, he would employ gold and gilt in profusion, for this colour symbolized the brightness of the sun. The lavish use of gold in which the picture itself finally becomes no more than a pretext for the frame can be observed in the 'Gate of the Tsar'; [page 85] this 'Gate' is the central panel of an iconostasis, which was a screen dividing the sanctuary of the Greek Orthodox churches from the lay part.

The churches of Russia vary greatly in size and shape, yet they are all unmistakably and uniquely Russian. The emotional and mystical nature of the Russian people, as well as the conflicting cultural influences in their vast land, find true expression in the strange brick, mortar and wood churches of Russia; their onion domes make them as characteristic in style as their Gothic counterparts in western Europe. The all-wooden Church of the Transfiguration at Kizhi [page 81], built without a single nail to keep the pieces together, has often been likened to a northern Taj Mahal, while the much simpler and more ancient church of Mary the Protector is distinctly Romanesque in the style of its windows and portals.

Religion in the Soviet Union of today is tolerated but definitely not encouraged. We all know that Marx called it 'the opium of the people'; the Russian Orthodox priests, hostile to the atheistic revolutionaries, were known as the 'Eyes of the Tsar' in pre-revolutionary Russia.

> *A priest arrives on trembling legs,*
> *shielding a relic in his hand . . .*
> *'Be off, you curly-headed priest!*
> *I'm a home-guardsman of the new life,*
> *and all that awaits you is the grave.'*

These words, written in 1927 by Zabolotsky, consigned religion and its priests to the grave a little prematurely. The various denominations and their representatives are still active, and even among the growing numbers of non-religious Soviet citizens there is an enduring respect for the wonderful Russian art which is an expression and a by-product of religious faith.

Pages 80-81
Kizhi on Lake Onega.
The twelve cupolas of the Church of the Transfiguration,
a masterpiece of Russian wooden architecture, dating
from about 1700.

Left: Icons from the Kizhi Church, showing Mary and the
Infant Christ, the Three Kings (left), the Shepherds
(right), and the Saints of Russia (below).

Page 82
The Pokrovskaya Church (Mary the Protector) on the
Nerl. One of the most beautiful examples of Romanesque
architecture in Russia, built at the end of the twelfth century.

Page 84
Icon of the 'Virgin of Kazan'.
It dates from the late period of Muscovite icon painting
in the sixteenth century.

Page 85
The 'Gate of the Tsar' (Tsarskie Vorota).
Centre panel of the Iconostasis in the Cathedral of the
Annunciation in the Kremlin.

The West: countryside and cities

The fields, forests and rivers of Russia have shaped the destiny of her people just as surely as the fact that England is an island has dictated the destiny of the English. The famous black earth or 'chernozem', a belt of rich soil hundreds of miles broad, runs from Siberia right across Russia, through the Ukraine and down to the Black Sea. It was down this belt that the Tartar hordes came galloping from the east to colonize the west and to change the course of its history. They fed their horses on the grass which grew twelve feet high on the fertile steppe which Russian farmers gradually turned into golden fields of wheat, maize and sunflowers.

> Ask me not why, but love I must
> Her fields' cold silences,
> Her sombre forests swaying in a gust
> Her rivers at the flood like seas.

The sombre, primeval forests of northern Russia shaped the character of its people; their architecture, their art and their artefacts were all hewn out of trees. The Russian child slept in a wooden cradle, played with wooden toys and learned to pray before a wooden icon. He shivered with terror at folk-tales about wolves and bears who lurked in the snowy forests all around, but he also learned to love and sing the beauty of his native trees, particularly the slender birch which holds such a special place in every Russian heart. These forests were Russia's first wealth, with their unlimited supply of timber and their many varieties of fur-bearing animals: the river-traders which Herodotus described in the fifth century, in the earliest reference to Russians on record, very probably brought rare furs to barter for Mediterranean silks and spices.

As for the great rivers which flow north, west, east and south, they are the true roads of Russian history; they have always nourished its soil and been its commercial life lines for internal and external trade. Perhaps no people in the world love their rivers quite as much as the Russians do. The Don and the Dnieper were the waterways to Greece and Byzantium, while the Volga led them farther east into Central Asia. The Volga is to Russia what the Nile is to Egypt: the ultimate source of life.

> My mother told me: my dear son,
> When all your roaming has been done,
> When you come home, fatigued but safe,
> Then dip your hands in a Volga wave.

Any Russian will tell you that you have not seen Russia until

you have seen the Volga, and he can sing you one of a dozen folk-songs which express his reverence and tenderness:

Lermontov's poem, *My Country*, captures the geographical essence of the 'real Russia' as distinct from the much larger Soviet Union of today. This Russia was the Holy Mother Russia so lovingly described by Russian poets and novelists of the nineteenth century; the attachment which these writers felt for their countryside has almost no equal in other literatures. If you go to Russia after reading Pushkin, Turgeniev, Tolstoy or Chekhov, you will recognize its fields, forests and rivers just from the vivid descriptions in their works. This Russia's eastern boundary was the great Steppe and the straight line of the Ural mountain chain, which was long regarded by the Russians as the limits of their known world. Its northern frontier was the ice-bound Sea of Barents. Towards the west, the brooding grey of the Baltic shielded it from the Nordic invaders while the Black Sea in the south gave it an opening onto the civilized world while western Europe was still in its Dark Ages. This Russia was studded by a triangle of great cities: the austere and grandiose St. Petersburg, Moscow with its 350 churches and its fringe orchards and Kiev, 'the mother of all Russian cities', deep in the heart of the Ukraine.

Lermontov speaks of his country's rivers as being 'at the flood like seas' which is not a poetic but a factual description. Those who live next to the mile-wide rivers rarely feel tempted to go to seaside resorts; they prefer instead to go into the land-bound countryside for their holidays, in order to get away from such vast masses of water. But no description of western Russia would be complete without a reference to its real seas. The Soviet Union is such a gigantic country and has frontiers with so many nations that we tend to forget that its coastline is twice the length of its land frontiers, that it is a great naval power and that a fair proportion of its natural wealth is drawn from its seas in nets. The Barents Sea can be dotted with ice-floes even in the summer months, while the waters of the Black Sea reach temperatures of 21°C (70°F), yet both are of definitely Russian flavour, with typically Russian cities like dour Murmansk on the Barents and the sunny, bustling port of Odessa on the Black Sea which is often described as the Russian Marseille. The main cities along the Baltic Coast are or were all capitals in their own right, and thus each one has its own special character: Leningrad, once the capital of Greater Russia; Tallinn, present capital of Estonia, and Riga, the capital of Latvia, are all major ports and important centres of the fishing industry; ancient church spires alternate along their skylines with the modern outlines of fishermen's collectives and the bustling cranes of

great docks. The many vessels which leave their harbours daily include not only trawlers but also monster factory ships, which are capable of canning 50 tons of fish, freezing 100 tons and manufacturing 120 tons of meal a day while fishing at sea. State-aided application of modern technology on such a scale explains why the Soviet fish catch doubles every ten years and is already two-and-a-half times greater than that of the United States.

The United States and Britain have never recognized the incorporation of the three Baltic republics, Estonia, Latvia and Lithuania, into the Soviet Union. This does not alter the fact that they had been a part of the Russian Empire since the eighteenth century and are thus very 'Russified'. During their brief period of independence as sovereign states, between 1918 and 1940, their economies stagnated; whereas now all three enjoy what is perhaps the highest standard of living in the Soviet Union. This atmosphere of prosperity as well as the beauty of their coastlines attracts tourists to the Baltic seaside resorts of Parnu and Balanga, despite the uncertain and chilly summer climate.

Bielorussia, on the borders of two of the Baltic Republics, has the misfortune to lie on the direct route from Berlin to Moscow – the classical invasion route. Because the name 'Bielo-Russia' means White Russia, many people still wrongly assume that the White Russian counter-revolutionaries, who fought against the 'Red' Communist forces, were natives of Bielorussia. In fact, the Republic is so named after the snowy-white garments made of flax which were worn by the Bielo-russian peasants. Pushkin was quite accurate when he said that the sheer size of Russia's boundaries 'drained the strength of all her invaders', but he neglected to add that this result was achieved at tremendous cost, not only to the invaders, but to those unlucky people living along the boundaries. 30,000 French soldiers died in a single battle near Minsk, capital of Bielorussia, during Napoleon's retreat from Moscow. Defeat on such a scale should have proved to the world that none could hope to invade Russia with impunity but the lesson was not learned conclusively. The statistics connected with Hitler's later invasion are terrifying: over 25 per cent of all Bielorussians were exterminated by the Nazis and there was not one but hundreds of Lidices and Oradours in this part of the Soviet Union. To this day, the population of Bielorussia is still below its pre-war level and the country looks somewhat poorer than the other Soviet republics. There are almost no relics of the past in this lovely land of dense forests, clear lakes, rivers and marshes. As it is the part of Russia which connects the great Russian plain to the rest of northern Europe, Bielorussia has echoed to the sound of marching boots, horse's hoofs and tanks so often in its history that almost all its cities and villages have been destroyed, not once but many times.

The Ukraine too had its share of wartime suffering: of Kiev's original population of 700,000, only some 120,000 people remained to greet the Soviet troops re-taking the city at the end of the last war. Yet the cheerfulness and vitality of the Ukrainian people, their good luck at having not only the best arable land in eastern Europe, but also the richest mineral resources in the European part of the Union, make it easier for them to dwell on the present and the future, rather than on the tragic past. To-day the land is covered with chestnut trees and poplar groves and the pretty thatched houses are often colour-washed in blue. As one traveller sensitively described the mixed industrial and rural landscape of the Ukraine: 'In the midst of orchards, plantations and immense sweeps of corn, great chimneys appear smoking fast and full like battleships steaming into action.'

Kiev, the capital of the Ukraine, is the cradle of Slavonic nationhood and Christianity. Moscow was not even a village at the time that Kiev was the capital of a flourishing state known as the Kiev Rus. It was famous throughout Europe as the centre of crafts, trade and culture. Repeated Mongol and Tartar invasions and later occupations by the Poles put an end to its power and wealth. The Muscovites were much further north and outside the path of invaders from east or west and their forests were as impregnable as castles. Its geographical location partially accounts for the fact that Moscow eventually became larger and more powerful than Kiev, although the latter is still the third largest city in the Soviet Union. It is now a beautiful modern city on a high bank of the Dnieper River, with spacious tree-lined avenues and many fascinating relics of the past, including the ancient cathedral of St. Sophia, which was built in 1036, soon after Christianity had been adopted by the Kievans. The architect's attempt to directly imitate St. Sophia in Constantinople did not quite succeed, and it was from this approximation to Byzantine masterpieces that the distinctive Russian style of church building later evolved. As Kiev is known as 'the mother of all cities', so St. Sophia can claim to be 'the mother of all Russian churches'.

Beyond the heavily industrialized Donetsk-Dnieper region with its vast coalfields and iron ore fields, beyond Kharkov with its giant lorry building plant, we reach the borders of Greater Russia and the long sweep of land between the Volga and the Don. Donetsk was once called Stalino, just as Volgograd was once called Stalingrad. But Stalins come and Stalins go while the rivers after which both towns were renamed continue to flow

Pages 98-99
In Bielorussia.
Wooden houses with television aerials on the roof crouch in the snow on both sides of a village street. In the country in Central Russia most houses are still built of wood.

Page 101
The Ukraine.
The straw-roofed peasant dwelling with its pump has become a rarity. Today collective farms and modern houses determine the character of the Ukrainian scene.

Pages 102-103
Murmansk.
The main fishing centre on the Barents Sea is the only harbour on the Soviet North Coast which remains ice-free throughout the winter. This city of 300,000 inhabitants, which has a School of Advanced Seamanship and a Research Institute of Fishing and Oceanography, gets its electricity supply from a tidal power station.

Pages 104-105
On the Baltic.
The coastal waters of the Soviet Baltic Republics,
Lithuania, Latvia and Estonia, are rich fishing
grounds.
Left: Lithuanian fisherman.
Right: Hauling in the nets on the high seas.

Pages 106-107
Tallinn, capital of the Estonian SSR.
In the Middle Ages a Hanseatic City, today an important
Baltic port and railway junction.
Our picture shows a view of the harbour and Cathedral
Hill with, on the right, the slim tower of the gothic Olai
Church.

Pages 108-109
Landscape between the Volga and the Don.
Fields of corn and grassy steppes stretch out endlessly into
the distance, broken only by lines of telegraph poles.

Page 111
The Collective Farm 'Nasha Rodina' (Our Motherland).
The peasants have formed their own agricultural
communities by uniting in collective farms.

Pages 112-113
Volgograd.
A new city arose from the ruins of devastated Stalingrad.
Our picture shows a view of the Volga.

Pages 114-115
Donetsk.
The regional capital of the Donbass, coalmining and
industrial centre in the east of the Ukrainian SSR.

Page 117
Kiev from the Old Town.
The Monument to the Cossack leader Bogdan
Khmelnitsky and, behind it, the three-storey bell tower of
the Cathedral of St. Sophia

Pages 118-119
Kiev, capital of the Ukraine.
The stone monument to Vladimir the Wise presiding over
the bright lights of the city on the banks of the Dnieper.

Siberia and the Far East

There are three facts which everyone knows about Siberia: that it is very big, very cold and very empty. It certainly is big: twice the size of Europe and forty-five times the size of the British Isles. And very cold: the mean January temperature in certain Siberian cities is −15°C (−5°F). What fewer people seem to know is that the summers can be hot, very hot by western European standards, easily 32°C (90°F) on certain days. Siberia is also very empty – only 25,000,000 people live there – but it does teem with life, if not with people. Its forests, known as 'taiga', swarm with red and silver foxes, sable, deer, elk, bears and wolves; it also contains two-thirds of the world's reindeer.

Another fact most people know about Siberia is that it is a place where people are sent involuntarily, without any desire to go there. The Siberian poet, Yevtushenko, spoke of his ancestors:

> . . . in exile here after a peasant's rising
> Here herded from the extremities of distance
> through mud and rain . . .

To be exiled to Siberia was a tragic fate. Many died, and some returned to Russia; others stayed on. Those who stayed had fallen in love with the land, just like the restless and the foot-loose and the dissatisfied people who had drifted there since the sixteenth century, not because they were forced to go, but because they were driven by the pioneer spirit and they found the challenge of so much emptiness irresistible. Siberia was then, as it is now, the land of opportunity, as was once the Far West of the United States. 'Go East!' was the slogan rather than 'Go West!' but the kind of people who went east to Siberia and west to California belonged to the same breed.

When one speaks of the eastern Soviet Union, it is difficult not to use adjectives like 'huge', 'immense' or 'gigantic'. But in attempting to define Siberia it is by means of absolute super-latives that it is best described. The biggest, the highest, the richest of everything. 'Rich' is a word which crops up over and over again in any description of this land. Its natural potential in coal, oil, ore, gold, uranium, lead, zinc, copper, diamonds, mercury and every other form of mineral wealth is almost terrifying in its implication of unjust distribution in a world increasingly depleted of raw materials. To quote a few statistics: Siberia's coal reserves could supply the whole world with coal for 2000 years. It probably contains more diamonds than all the mines of South Africa. Nuggets of gold weighing up to 31 pounds have been found there. There are 75 acres of forest for every inhabitant of Siberia. Lake Baikal, the deepest and oldest

120

lake in the world, is also the largest reservoir of fresh water, containing nearly 20 per cent of all such water on earth. The briefest study of Siberia's economic potential will convince anyone that this region's future is dazzling. Many people who would once have considered living in Siberia a fate worse than death might now cast an envious glance at that part of the globe.

When we speak of the achievements of the Soviet Union as a whole, we speak of its present and of what has been accomplished in the recent past, or of what is being done right now to translate many an ambitious dream into a living reality in the immediate future. It is much harder to do this in the case of Siberia. This is the country of the future, often of the distant future that even our children may not live to see. To be wildly enthusiastic about Siberia, one has to be inspired, like the poet Mayakovsky, by the future. Not that Siberia's present achievements are negligible: it already has the biggest power station in the world and not satisfied with possessing one of the world's greatest natural lakes, it now also has the largest man-made lake at Bratsk. Besides manufacturing the mightiest hydro-electric turbines in the world, it contains an impressive quantity of heavy industries, a fact which probably saved the Soviet Union during World War II when so much of its western territory was occupied by the enemy. Although it has only 10 per cent of the country's population, Siberia grows 25 per cent of the Soviet Union's grain harvest in vast state farms.

Maps of Siberia become out of date very quickly, as great new cities spring up along the banks of its rivers and lakes:

> *Suddenly lit up with millions of lights,*
> *the elements of the un-coordinated world*
> *now synchronized in one harmonious choir.*

And yet it is still the future which most excites the imagination, for as yet the surface has hardly been scratched. The very climate of Siberia may have to be altered before much of its wealth can be exploited, yet even that is considered feasible by the inhabitants of some Siberian cities, where scientists work night and day to overcome all natural obstacles. When we consider that Siberia is floating on a sea of oil and what that asset implies in our oil-starved future, we understand how prophetic Lomonosov was when he declared many years ago: 'Russian might will grow as Siberia develops.' If, as some predict, the Soviet Union will outstrip the United States as the world's foremost economic and political giant in the twenty-first century, it will owe much of its eventual supremacy to the infinite resources of Siberia.

Pages 122-123
Siberian Taiga.
The most extensive zone of vegetation in the USSR is the pine forest belt of the Taiga. The mighty Irtysh and other swiftly flowing rivers flow north through the forests which are still almost untouched by civilization.

Pages 124-125
Forest Tundra.
The permanently frozen soil of Northern Siberia, on which only the top surface thaws in the summer. The sparse vegetation of the Tundra mosses, reeds and dwarf trees are all the nourishment there is for the wandering herds of reindeer.

Pages 126-127
Reindeer Herd.
The natives of the Siberian north live mainly by keeping reindeer. The Eveni and the Orochi are particularly famous as reindeer herdsmen.

Page 129
Kamchatka, Land of Volcanoes.
The earth has not yet settled down on the Pacific peninsula – hot springs, bubbling cauldrons of mud, geysers and fire-belching volcanoes recall the origins of our planet.
This aerial photograph shows in the foreground the crater-edge of the volcano Krashennikov; and behind, the summit of another volcano, Kronotsky (3528 metres).

Pages 130-131
The Amur.
The river which divides the USSR from China. The great artery of the Far East, already 2 kilometres wide at Khabarovsk, flows 4354 kilometres to the Pacific and is therefore longer than the Volga.

Pages 132-133
Krasnoyarsk.
*The biggest power station in the world produces almost
6 million kilowatt-hours. The dam, which creates a vast
lake from the Yenisei River, is 124 metres high.*

Pages 134-135
The Trans-Siberian Railway.
*Connects Moscow with the Pacific harbour of Vladivostok.
The line, almost 10,000 kilometres long, is now largely
electrified. Between Ufa and Chelyabinsk it crosses the
Urals.*

Page 137
A girl from the Tuvin Tribe.
*The people of the Tuvin Autonomous Republic are among
the ancient inhabitants of Siberia.*

Pages 138-139
Iron Ore Mining.
*The mineral resources of the USSR seem inexhaustible!
In Western Siberia the Kursk Magnetic Anomaly alone
yields 80 to 90 million tons of iron ore annually. Much of
the high grade ore is found in shallow deposits and can be
mined by open-cast methods.*

The South: landscapes and people

If some inhabited parts of the Soviet Union have the worst climate in the world, some have just about the best and those are the very ones we know the least about. We have all heard about Russia's snow and wolves and of the fatal 'General Winter' which defeats every would-be conqueror. How many of us know anything of the Russia which lies on the same parallel as Central Greece and Southern Italy? A Russia where roses and mimosa bloom in winter, where citrus groves and tea plantations thrive, where there is uninterrupted sunshine 200 days of the year, a land of plenty, of fruit and of wine, a place where the inhabitants enjoy life so much that they cannot bear to die and thus have the highest proportion of centenarians in the world. When we try to visualize a typical Soviet citizen, we picture him in a fur coat and boots, with a grim and gloomy expression on his face which comes from his permanent struggle against a harsh environment. And indeed, what would our shivering northern Russian do without his south? It is his one golden glimpse of a *joie de vivre* which cannot exist in very cold climates, whether in the USSR or elsewhere. It is his passport to physical well-being: he can eat fruit from Moldavia when his own orchards are under snow. He can warm himself drinking boiling hot tea from Georgia with a slice of Georgian lemon. He can celebrate a happy occasion with southern champagnes and wines, or cheer himself up on a long, dark evening with a glass of Armenian cognac.

The 'Russian South' is a climatic rather than a geographic entity. The Republic of Moldavia belongs to this south, as does the southernmost tip of the Ukraine and the Crimean peninsula. The greater part of the south, however, is Transcaucasia, the area which lies on the far side of the Caucasus Mountains. These mountains form a fabulously beautiful and rugged chain which stretches between the Black Sea and the Caspian Sea. They are like an unbroken wall in a great crusader fortress, with the occasional high turret of a mountain peak; forty of these peaks rise to a height of over 10,000 feet. Mount Elbrus is the highest of these 'towers' and, at 18,481 feet, the tallest mountain in Europe. As there are only two usable passes across the entire range, it is not surprising that 'for millennia the Caucasus served as an enormous comb lying on the migration route from Asia to Europe'. So many groups got stranded in the comb that today the Caucasus is the home of at least 50 different nationalities, ranging from the descendants of medieval crusaders who lost their way in the mountains to the strange tribes of 'Caucasian Negroes'.

The Caucasus is varied not only ethnographically, but also geographically. Many peoples speaking many languages live

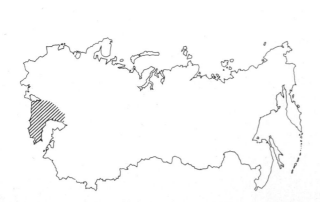

together in many settings. Armenia is barren enough in parts to be known as 'Karaskan', or the land of rocks, while the high plateaux of Georgia are extremely fertile and the sub-tropical vegetation along the Black Sea coast is luxuriant with eucalypti, oleanders, yucca, walnut and laurel. But the Caucasus has two constants in its variety: it is all mountainous and all beautiful. This is one of the beauty spots of the world and Russian authors have been inspired by its scenery ever since this cluster of small countries became part of the Russian Empire in the early nineteenth century. In a region so beautiful, it did not seem possible to improve on nature and the favourite colours of the famous Azerbaijani artists were blue, green and brown, the colours of the land itself. In Erivan, the capital of Armenia, only the local volcanic stone has been used for construction so that every building seems to sprout from the earth itself in 90 distinct shades, ranging from jet black to the subtle pink of a wild rose. As though to match the beauty of their natural environment, the tall, straight Georgians are reputed to be one of the handsomest races on earth.

The Caucasus has an older recorded human history than any other part of the Soviet Union. Homer sang the praises of the Georgian wines and Erivan celebrated its 2750th anniversary in 1968, which makes it one of the oldest cities in the world. Kabystan's sheer cliffs and rocks are covered with petroglyphics dating as far back as 8000 BC, which was the very dawn of civilization. Whoever speaks of an old human history speaks of many wars and massacres and an endless succession of battles. The history of this part of the world has been turbulent; its people have fought back Romans, Turks, Persians, Arabs and Mongols. Yet no amount of fighting to defend their mountain strongholds could ever dampen the high spirits of these warrior races. The statue of Mother Georgia outside Tbilisi expresses the duality of these warrior peoples. She holds a cup of wine in one hand and a sword in the other. The wine symbolizes hospitality to all who come in friendship, while the sword symbolizes the fierce determination to resist enemies. The very spirit of the people and of the land is there: generous, expansive and glad to share their plenty, yet still untamed and fierytempered, and ever ready to defend their national honour and their beautiful mountain home.

Pages 142-143
Combine Harvesters in formation.
The grain harvest is fully mechanized with half a million combine harvesters in action in the fields of the state and collective farms.

Pages 144-145
Tea Harvest in Georgia.
'Sakhartvelo', the tea-harvesting machine developed by Soviet engineers, picks 150 kilograms of tea leaves per hour.

Pages 146-147
The Crimea.
Mountain slopes rise up from the sea like a great amphitheatre. Famous vineyards lie among the white cliffs.

Pages 148-149
Armenian Mountain Landscape.
Karaskan, Land of Rocks, is the Armenians' name for their homeland. Sheep and mountain goats graze on chalky slopes.

Page 150
Mount Elbrus in the Great Caucasus Range is, at 5633 metres, the highest mountain in Europe. Its summit is covered with snow and ice at all times of the year.

Page 151
Wine Growers in the Moldavian SSR.

Page 153
Tbilisi (Tiflis)
Capital of the Georgian SSR, founded 1500 years ago by King Vachtang Gorgasali.
Our picture shows the fifth-century Metechi Church and houses of the Old Town above the rocky gorge of the kura.

Central Asia: landscapes and people

Perhaps Rudyard Kipling was right when he made his famous statement that 'East is East and West is West and never the twain shall meet,' yet if there ever has been a crossroad where East met West, it was in that part of Central Asia once known as Russian Turkestan. A glance at the map will suffice to show us why a city like Samarkand could once be referred to as 'the navel of the world'. It was the hub of caravan routes from India and China, a resting place and a gateway to the West, on the long, long journey from Cathay to the Mediterranean. It was in Bukhara that Marco Polo, the adventurer from the West, stopped on his way to China. He described the city as 'very noble and great' which it must have been with its 100 religious colleges and its 400 mosques, in the days when it was the far Northern outpost of the Moslem faith and its cathedral mosque, Bibi Khanum, was one of the largest and most famous Islamic temples in the world. Even today the cities of Tashkent and Alma-Ata are logical meeting places for all the different Soviet nationalities; students from Asia, Africa and Latin America come to these cities' educational establishments in even greater numbers than to Moscow. The Republics of Central Asia are the Soviet Union's logical link with all the countries of Asia, just as Leningrad was and still is the logical link with northern Europe.

The history of this part of the world is one of great armies marching to conquer new dominions; the names of those who overran the kingdoms of Central Asia come straight out of the pages of a child's history book. The Persian king, Cyrus, conquered these lands and Alexander the Great drove out the Persians 300 years later. Roman legions swept across the Karakum desert, followed later by Turks and by Arabs. Genghis Khan, on his way to the terror-stricken West, devastated the area so thoroughly that it was almost completely depopulated. Later, it was Tamerlaine who raced his golden hordes across the red and black deserts and made Samarkand his capital, determined to rebuild it 'like no other city in the world'. Central Asia is still inhabited by the descendants of his mounted warriors who defeated all the armies from the west for centuries.

But the history of this part of the world goes much further back than Alexander. The Amu Darya and Syr Darya basins of Central Asia's two great rivers are among the oldest inhabited places in the world. Archaeologists have discovered traces of highly developed civilizations which were comparable to Mesopotamia, Egypt, Babylon and Assyria, possessing thriving agricultures and using artificial irrigation over 3000 years ago.

The various civilizations which succeeded one another had

all long lain in ruins by the time Russia annexed Turkestan in 1865. The area was so backward that pre-revolutionary Russian sociologists predicted it would take 2500 years for its peoples to catch up with the modern world. The fabled Samarkand, the city whose bazaar had once been crammed with silks, gold and gems of every colour, was now almost a ghost town with only 15,000 inhabitants; its splendid mosques and mausoleums were crumbling into dust. The social structure and the living conditions of the people were medieval. Slaves were still sold in the markets. The literacy rate was only 2 percent for men and practically nonexistent for the women, who were little better off than slaves. Hunger, disease and dirt were the common lot and fewer than two children in ten lived to be one year old. The whole vast country was one of wastelands and deserts, scantily peopled by primitive nomadic tribes.

The Tsar's administrators did little to alter this state of affairs; apart from putting up a few buildings and sending reluctant military personnel and immigrants to a string of dusty garrison towns, they did not interfere with the local customs or with the economy. It was not until after the Bolshevik Revolution that conditions started to alter. To begin with, Turkestan was split up into five autonomous republics: Kazakhstan, Uzbekistan, Tadjikistan, Turkmenia and Kirghisia. This breakdown of the land into separate units along rational geographic and ethnic lines made obvious sense. The original Russian Turkestan was unmanageably large and even now the single republic of Kazakhstan is four times the size of Texas, while the other republics are all of a respectable size by any standard.

A combination of irrigation, compulsory education, the development of natural resources and the full emancipation of women achieved a miracle on a scale comparable to the accomplishments of Communist China, in its most backward regions. This is the land of the Great Leap Forward, where one can marvel, whatever one's political persuasion, at the way human organization and effort can bridge the gap of centuries, can make the desert bloom, can reconcile the past with the present, can turn the little starvelings of yesteryear into healthy, smiling schoolchildren and the black-veiled women into comrade bulldozer drivers. Cotton, wheat, rice, sugar-beet, tobacco and fruit now grow where musical desert winds used to blow. Barges and motorboats sail down broad irrigation canals, where only cocoa-coloured camels would once have dared to venture. Even the Kirghiz and Uzbek nomads who have refused to settle down, because nomads everywhere like to keep on the move however attractive the alternative, are being 'collectivized' in ways that make their life more pleasant and more productive.

When they pack up their yurtas, or felt tents, to set off with their flocks of fleecy Karakul sheep, they are followed about by mobile schools, dispensaries, shops, film projectors and by what the Russians quaintly call 'zoo-technicians', that is what we call prosaically 'vets'. The gasfields, oilfields and coalfields of Central Asia have brought industrial wealth and might to cities like Tashkent and orchard-ringed Alma-Ata, the 'Mother of Apples'. The millions of acres which have been reclaimed from wasteland make these republics a sort of Holland in reverse. Holland took its fields out of the water by pushing back the sea, whereas the Russians have pushed the desert back by bringing in water from the Amu and the Syr rivers. The result is that 75 different varieties of cotton are grown in Uzbekistan alone, making it the third largest cotton producer in the world, after such giants as the USA and China.

The republics of Central Asia are only one of the many economic success stories of the Soviet style of administration, though they are perhaps its greatest success story to date because the Great Leap Forward had to be made across a chasm of so many centuries. But what is unique and belongs only to this part of the world is its collection of superb relics recalling a past which was often glorious, however bloodthirsty, and an exotic way of life which has survived to this day. For the past is extraordinarily alive in Central Asia, perhaps too much so, according to some people. As one traveller wrote: 'The past still lies heavily on the face of the land and in the spirit of the native-born peoples. They have trafficked for so long in the stuff of history that neither the present nor indeed the future can remove a certain paralysis with which the brilliant memory of their past obsesses them.'

There remains much of the Arabian Nights in the cities like Bukhara and Khiva, with their narrow alleys, their clay and brick oriental houses with ochre-coloured roofs, their bright blue-domed mosques and their many men and women who wear traditional silk and cotton robes. Men sitting crosslegged and drinking tea in a bazaar, wearing *tuibiteika*, the national black and white-patterned skull-caps, men who are deeply absorbed in Moslem rites of prayer, a camel rider who could be a contemporary of Tamerlaine's golden hordes rather than one of their descendants, even a Koranic school which is still so active, not a mere monument to an outdated way of life. Indeed, it is not only the seat of the spiritual head of all Soviet Muslims but also one of the foremost centres of Islamic culture in the world.

What fascinates visitors to the Central Asian republics, however, is not so much the living traditions and ancient customs that can still be found here, but the great monuments of the past. Chinese, Mongol, Indian, Persian, Afghan, Turkish and Tibetan influences subtly merge in these buildings to create a discreet blend of beauty. Samarkand, Bukhara and Khiva are museum cities of ornate .palaces, mosques and mausoleums. Each glance down their ancient alleys is like turning a page in a catalogue of Islamic treasures. The unique mausoleums built between the thirteenth and fifteenth century include the tomb of the great Tamerlaine himself. Jade, turquoise, mosaics and ornamented tiles in vivid colours were used in exquisite patterns to decorate the interiors and exteriors of buildings, which are all marvels of Moslem religious architecture.

One of the most interesting aspects of Soviet society is the care it has lavished on retaining what is best about the past, while gradually eliminating that which is felt to have no place in progressive society. It has broken the power of the religious fanatics who once misruled this land, but it has also restored the ruined mosques with fanatical patience and put each tiny glazed tile back in its proper place. It has swept away filthy slums while rebuilding palaces. It has torn away the women's veils yet encouraged their beautiful and comfortable traditional silk costumes. It has educated its citizens to appreciate and to work for a better way of life, but at all times it has helped them, by a variety of measures, to retain a strong sense of national identity. Perhaps nowhere is this policy more apparent than in the Republics of Central Asia; it is here that people should go who still believe that conformity and standardization are the outstanding features of the Soviet administration.

Pages 156-157
The Hour of Prayer.
The earliest inhabitants of Samarkand, the Uzbeks and the Tadzhiks, are devotees of the teaching of Mohammed.

Page 158
In the Bazaar in Samarkand.
As our fathers once lived, so we live now.
Tea-drinking in the Chaihana is for the men. They drink green tea from plain cups and discuss the day's news.

Page 159
Samarkand in Uzbekistan.
In 1369 the Mongol Khan Timur, called Tamerlaine by the Russians, made this the capital city of his empire.
The tombs of the Shah-i-Zinda Necropolis are among the magnificent buildings dating from that period.

Pages 160-161
*The Pamirs, also known as 'the Roof of the World', are
the meeting-point of three nations, the USSR, China and
Afghanistan. The massive range contains the two highest
points in the Soviet Union, Communism Peak
(7495 metres) and Lenin Peak (7134 metres).*

Pages 166-167
*The Karakum Desert.
Turkmenistan is the hottest and driest area of Central
Asia; three-fifths of the land is desert. An 850-kilometre-long
canal cuts through the Karakum Desert from Amu Darya
to Ashkabad. It is planned to extend it to the Caspian Sea.
Left: Camel riders of the Erzeri tribe.*

Pages 168-169
*The complex called Neftyannye Kamni (Oil-bearing
Rocks) was set up 40 kilometres from the coast on steel pillars to
exploit underwater oil reserves in the Caspian Sea.*

USSR science and technology

Russia was an extremely backward and underdeveloped country in the final years of the Tsarist regime, especially in comparison with the other nations of Europe. It was not a 'poor' country; with its many natural assets, it was a very rich country, but it was a rich country full of poor people. It has been estimated that at the time of the Revolution well over three-quarters of the Russian population lived badly, by any modern standards, and this state of affairs was due not only to inequalities in the distribution of the national wealth, though these were extreme, but also to Russia's very low level of economic development. In a land of lakes, streams and rivers, there were periodic droughts and consequent famines in many areas. The lack of industry meant little foreign trade or economic prosperity for the cities, despite vast mineral resources. Although there was a great deal of arable land per inhabitant, yields were low because of inefficient and unscientific farming methods. Inadequate transport facilities led to serious food shortages in the towns, even when harvests were good; the protests of hungry workers of Leningrad and other cities, demonstrating in front of empty food shops in 1916, which did much to bring about the collapse of the *ancien regime*, sprang from economic more than political problems.

Most of the answers to the economic problems which beset Russia after the Revolution lay not just in the reorganization of the means of production, but also in achieving rapid and wide-scale advances in technology. It was logical, given the great potential of the land itself, that the leaders of the new Soviet State should turn to science as to a saviour, which would emancipate the Russian people from a life of poverty and drudgery. The notion that applied science and technology would be the salvation of mankind was very much in keeping with Marxist doctrine and its strongly humanistic-materialistic philosophy. Writers like Chekhov had already sensed that science might one day take the place of religion as a more modern spiritual aspiration, which would nonetheless be suited to the traditionally mystical side of the Russian character. In one of his short stories an engineer has a deeply emotional experience as he gazes at some electric lights and new railway tracks, where before there was only a wilderness. His heart almost bursts with enthusiasm as he realizes the significant role that scientific progress could play in the lives of his fellow men. This mystique of science has persisted throughout the twentieth century. Russia has passed from the coal age into the age of electricity and from the atomic age into the space age, but the prestige of its scientists has not diminished nor their achievements questioned in the way that it has become fashionable to

170

question the benefits of technological progress in the West. This enduring faith in all things scientific has even been extended to the machine itself; from the modest tractor to the giant electronic computer, it is not only the man who operates it, but the machine which also commands respect and affection. The Soviet writer, Paustovsky, once declared: 'You must write about machines as you write about people – feeling their pulse-beat, loving them, penetrating into their life. I always feel physical pain when a machine is abused.'

It is accepted that the Soviet Union would probably have been defeated by Germany in World War II had it not developed its industry and agriculture, making giant strides in technology between 1921 and 1941. This consciousness was further to enhance the heroic and patriotic image of Soviet science and scientists. The ordinary Russian knew that he owed victory nearly as much to his country's technological progress, to the extension of its rail network and to the expansion of its metallurgic and mining industries, as to the bravery of the Soviet armies. What is perhaps not so often realized in the West is how much the Cold War consolidated this feeling. After 1945, the Soviet people deeply feared and distrusted their powerful and more advanced American rival. They suspected during the interval of several years between the development of the American atomic bombs and the Russian that the United States might be tempted to take advantage of so devastating a superiority to wage a 'preventative' war against them. So when Russian physicists finally developed an atomic bomb, a hydrogen bomb and an impressive range of intercontinental ballistic missiles, the Soviet people felt safe.

It was now, more than ever before, that scientists rather than military men seemed to be the great defenders of Mother Russia. The development of an ambitious space exploration programme in the late 'fifties coincided with a renewed interest in the outside world. Such exploits as the launching of the first Sputnik and the historic flight of Yuri Gagarin enormously enhanced Soviet prestige abroad at a time when the USSR was growing eager for international recognition of its scientific achievements after years of isolation.

Today, those achievements are fully recognized by other nations. The world has acknowledged the fact that the USSR has an extremely highly developed scientific organization, with over 4000 research institutes and laboratories working in every branch of the economy. They admire the Soviet Union's very high ratio of doctors and engineers, while advocates of women's liberation can point out that nearly three-quarters of all Soviet doctors and a third of the graduate engineers are women.

171

Pages 172-173
Voskhod I.
The rocket which powered the first manned spacecraft is now exhibited in honour of the pioneers of space travel.

Pages 174-175
Yuri Gagarin and a model of the Voskhod I rocket which carried his capsule into space.

Pages 176-177
Tu-144 in the Wind Tunnel.
The world's first supersonic airliner made its maiden flight on December 31st 1968.

Pages 178-179
The Cyclotron.
The magnet of the ion accelerator in Dubna. It uses as much energy as is produced by a medium-sized power station.

Page 181
The Laboratory for the Physiology and Pathology of Old Age in Kiev is concerned with experimental work in the fields of gerontology and geriatrics.

Pages 182-183
Centre for Atomic Research in Dubna.
This town of physicists established north of Moscow in 1956 now has a population of 50,000.

Pages 184-185
The elements provide as harsh a challenge as any to Soviet technology.

Page 188
The future for Russia;
young scientists during lectures at Akademgorod in Siberia.

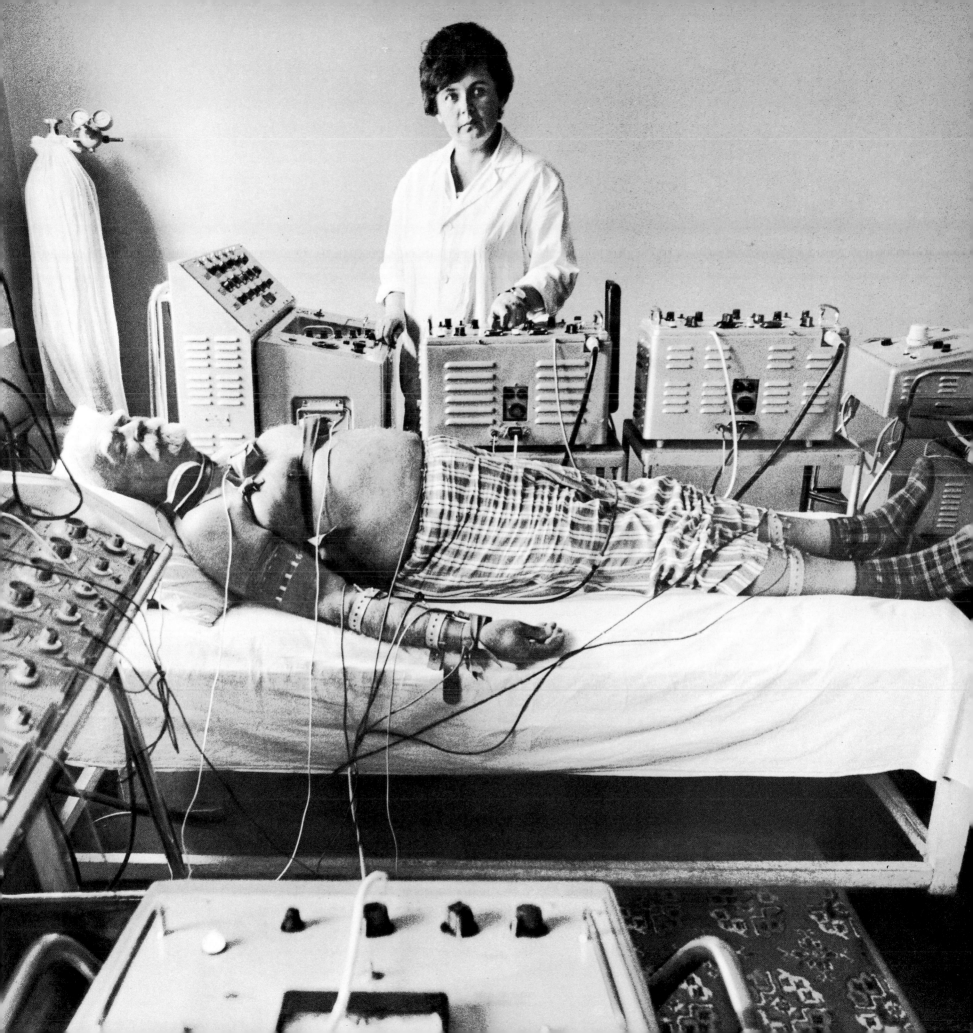

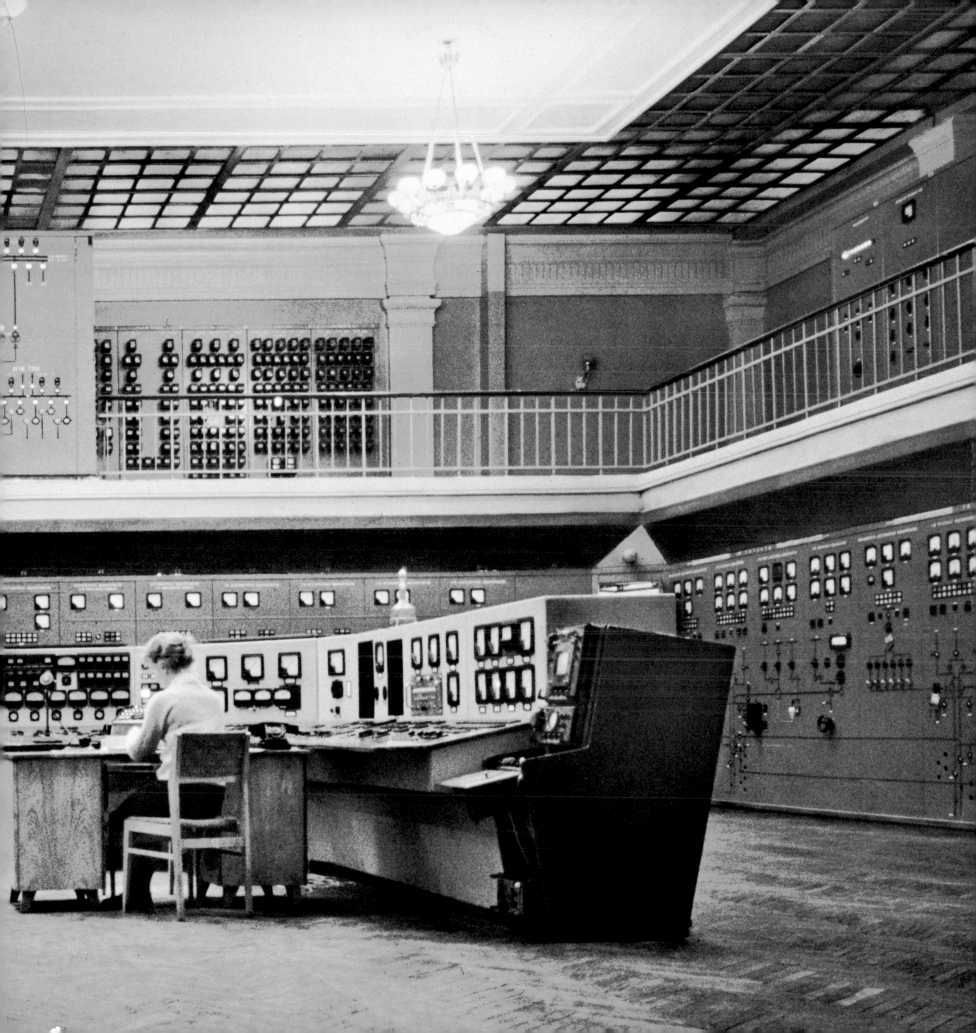

CZECHOSLOVAKIA

HUNGARY

POLAND

ROMANIA

BALTIC SEA

FINLAND

BARENTS SEA

Murmansk

9 Vilna

Riga **4**

Tallinn

8

Leningrad

Minsk

3

10

Odessa

Kiev

12

Dnieper

Moscow

Archangelsk

U R A L S

Ob

Irtysch

BLACK SEA

Don

11

Volga

Volgograd

5

Tbilisi

1

2

2

Baku

Astrakhan

CASPIAN SEA

U R A L

Chelyabinsk

Omsk

Tomsk

TURKEY

ARAL SEA

6

IRAN

Amu-Darya

15

13

Lake Balkhash

Samarkand

Tashkent

Alma-Ata

7

AFGHANISTAN

14

Republics of the USSR

1 Armenia   4 Estonia

2 Azerbaijan   5 Georgia

3 Bielorussia   6 Kazakhstan

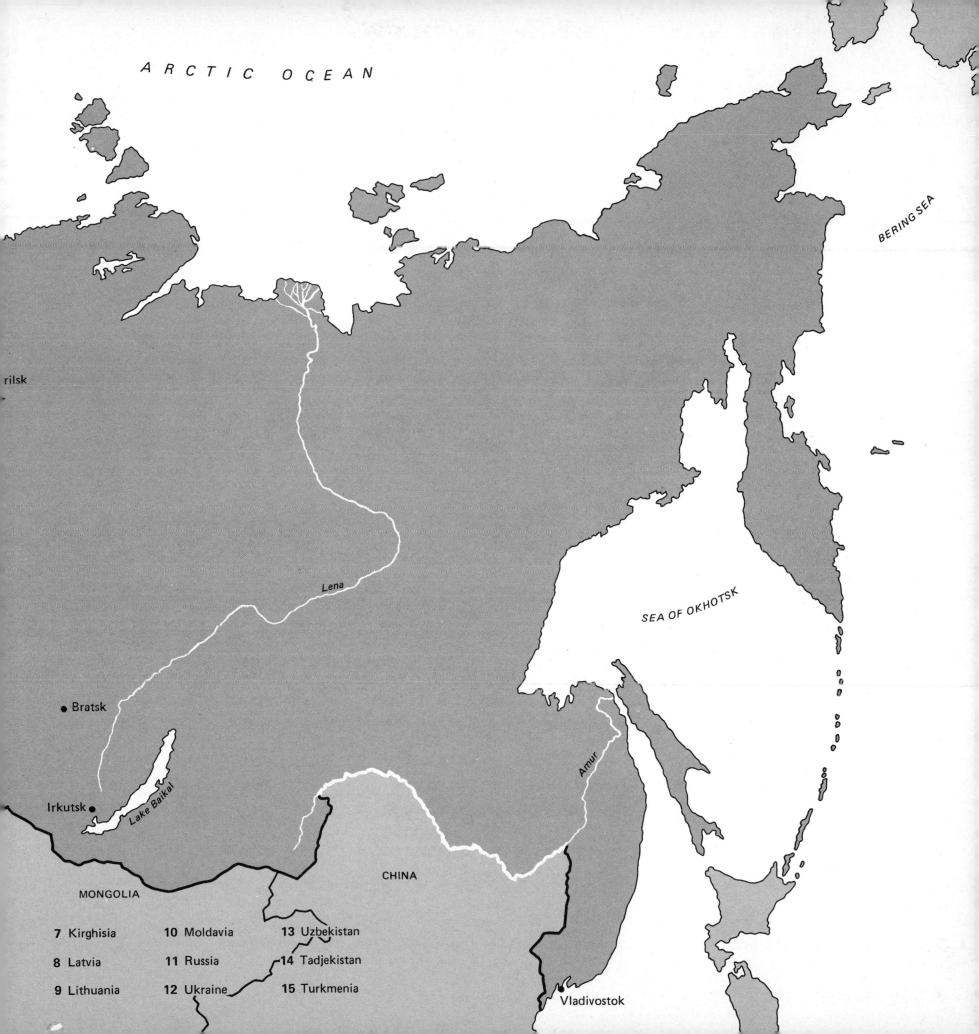

ARCTIC OCEAN

BERING SEA

rilsk

Lena

SEA OF OKHOTSK

Bratsk

Amur

Irkutsk

Lake Baikal

CHINA

MONGOLIA

Vladivostok

7 Kirghisia	10 Moldavia	13 Uzbekistan
8 Latvia	11 Russia	14 Tadjekistan
9 Lithuania	12 Ukraine	15 Turkmenia

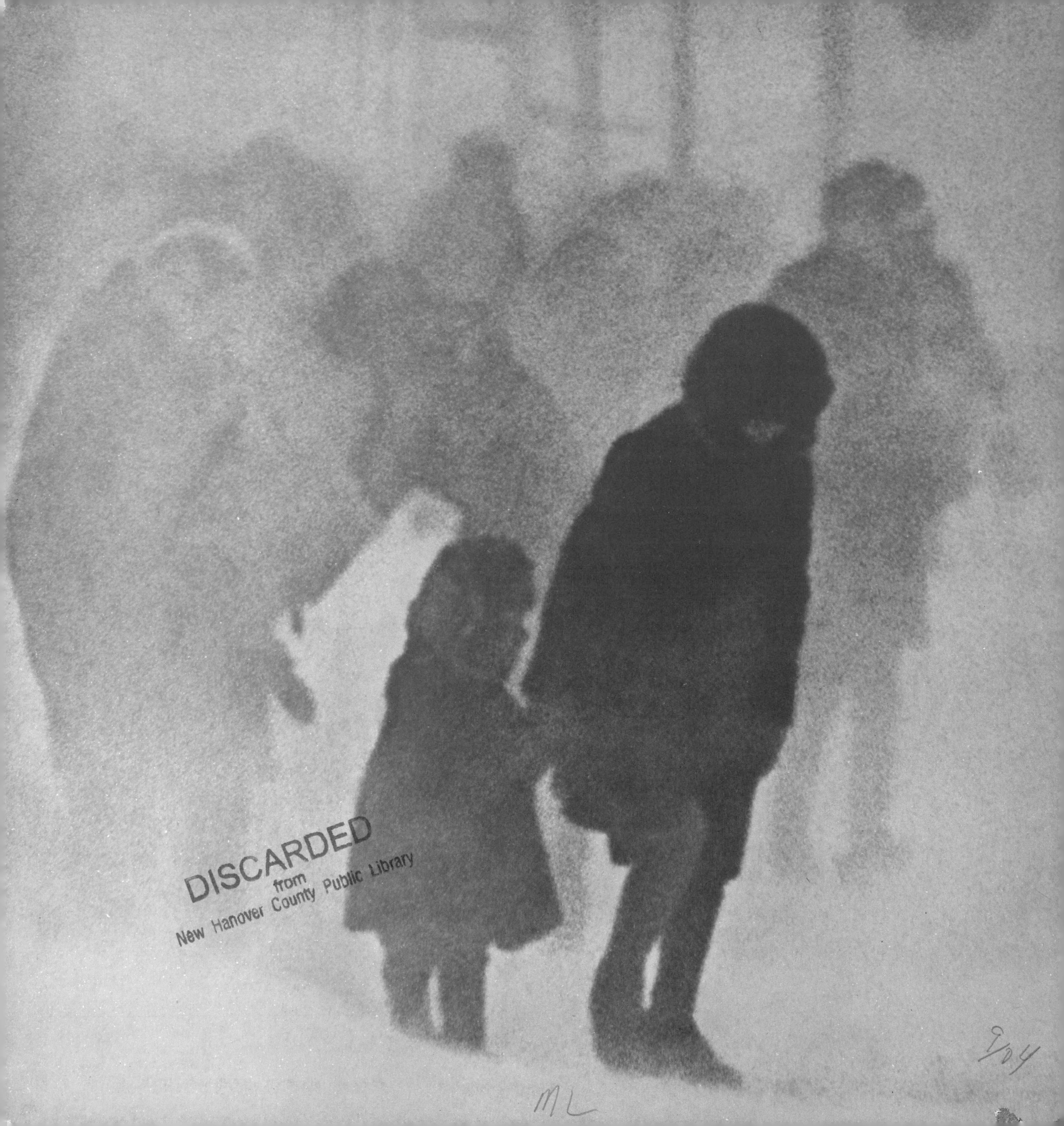